SUITABILITY AND SECURITY PROCESSES REVIEW
REPORT TO THE PRESIDENT

EXECUTIVE SUMMARY

I0411015

INTRODUCTION

In the Fall of 2013, the President directed the Office of Management and Budget (OMB) to conduct a 120-day review of Federal employee suitability and contractor fitness determinations as well as security clearance procedures. This Review complimented related efforts of the Department of Defense (DoD) with respect to physical and personnel security and of the National Security Council (NSC) and OMB on access to and security of classified information.

This work was carried out by the Suitability and Security Clearance Performance Accountability Council (PAC). Chaired by OMB's Deputy Director for Management, the PAC includes the Director of National Intelligence (DNI) and the Director of the Office of Personnel Management (OPM), in their respective roles as Security and Suitability Executive Agents (see Appendix A). The Senior Review Panel (hereafter referred to as the Panel), comprised of representatives from OMB, ODNI, OPM, DoD, Department of Homeland Security (DHS), Department of Justice (DOJ), the Federal Bureau of Investigation (FBI), and the Information Security Oversight Office (ISOO), as well as representatives from the NSC, drove an intensive interagency review to assess risks inherent in the current security, suitability, and credentialing processes and identify recommended solutions to safeguard our personnel and protect our nation's most sensitive information.

The Review addressed suitability and security investigations for civilian, military, and contractor personnel. The same investigative and adjudicative standards apply to both Federal employees and contractors who receive clearances, as the work to protect our national security is no less critical when the work is performed by contractors. The Review also examined the work performed by each group in conducting these investigations. The current practice of utilizing contract investigators to collect relevant information is an appropriate practice and consistent with regulations, provided the necessary oversight, metrics, and controls are in place. Our recommendations include improvements in the areas of contractor oversight, accountability, and quality metrics going forward.

This Report presents a set of recommendations that establish new priorities for reform, while accelerating efforts already underway. These priorities include improving access to relevant information, especially state and local law enforcement records, and accelerating the shift to a continuous evaluation model across government; improving risk management approaches to reduce vulnerabilities in our current processes, including reduction of the total number of clearance holders and the backlog of periodic reinvestigations; and improving enterprise operations, to include strengthening oversight and government-wide implementation efforts while effectively managing limited resources. As part of its ongoing responsibilities, the PAC will be accountable for driving these changes and holding agencies accountable for implementing approved recommendations.

This Report first gives an overview of the current processes for conducting investigations and adjudications of all categories of personnel, and then summarizes the key conclusions and recommendations of the Panel, concluding with proposed next steps.

OVERVIEW OF CURRENT PROCESSES

Government vetting processes generally involve two distinct activities: *investigation activities* which include application and information collection; and *adjudication activities* which include information assessment and decision making. A security investigation is defined as any investigation required for eligibility to hold a sensitive national security position or access to classified information by military, civilian, or government contractor personnel performing work for, or on behalf of, the government.

The Review also addressed background investigations that support hiring, credentialing, suitability, and fitness decisions. OPM conducts approximately 95 percent of the total background investigations government-wide. There are 21 other agencies, many within the Intelligence Community authorized to conduct their own background investigations, which accounts for the remaining 5 percent.

There are different levels of investigation depending on the level of risk, position sensitivity, or access requirements. Clearance determinations remain valid for a specified number of years after the completion of the investigation. Periodic reinvestigation cycles established pursuant to Executive Order, are as follows[1]:

> ➢ Every 5 years for a Top Secret (TS) clearance or access to sensitive compartmented information (TS/SCI)
> ➢ Every 10 years for a Secret clearance
> ➢ Every 15 years for a Confidential clearance

Revised standards for suitability and national security investigations were approved by the PAC in 2012, and are in the process of being implemented. Full implementation is currently planned for 2017. The revised standards align investigative elements at each tier (see Appendix B) to promote efficiency, consistency, and employee and contractor mobility across different government agencies thereby improving reciprocity and reducing program costs. The standards at each level of investigation also now build upon, but do not duplicate one another. This ensures investigative requirements previously satisfied are not checked again just because an individual moves to a position requiring a higher level of investigation.

Investigations to support a Secret level security clearance include automated and manual checks of criminal history, terrorist activities, credit, and foreign activities and influence. When the checks identify issues of concern, additional checks, including interviews and other more manual efforts, are conducted as needed. TS/SCI investigations add non-automated checks, including

---

[1] Executive Order 12968 "Access to Classified Information" signed August 2, 1995

interviews of the subject, employers, and social references, and collect information related to foreign influence and foreign preference.

Currently, OPM relies heavily on contract investigators to perform much of the information collection in the background investigation process. OPM then performs a quality review and assembles the completed investigation and transmits it to the requesting agency for adjudication. Non-OPM conducted investigations, largely in the Intelligence Community, also use a mix of contractors and Federal employees to gather information.

All adjudication decisions are inherently governmental functions and are conducted by Federal employees in the agency where the individual will be assigned. The agency adjudicator assigned to an investigation will review it using applicable guidelines relative to hiring, credentialing, and/or security clearance determinations. When determining eligibility for access to classified information, adjudicators use the National Security Adjudicative Guidelines to either make a favorable decision or to identify disqualifying information and deny or revoke the clearance.

Executive branch-wide policy directs agencies to minimize the number of employees and contractors with eligibility for access to classified information to the minimum required to conduct agency functions. Still, the number of clearance-eligible personnel is considerable, exceeding 5.1 million including civilian and military employees and contractors in Fiscal Year 2013 (See Table 1). Of that number, only 60 percent had access to classified information.[2]

Table 1: Number of employees/contractors both eligible[3] and in access in FY2013 by clearance level

	Confidential/Secret				Top Secret				Total Eligible
	Gov't	Contractor	Other	Total	Gov't	Contractor	Other	Total	
Eligible Staff*	2,886,106	558,626	175,859	3,620,591	851,920	497,683	180,185	1,529,788	**5,150,379**
% in access	41.7%	83.7%	82.2%	50%	76%	91%	98%	83.4%	**60%**

*As of 10/1/13

Background investigations accrue significant expenses for agencies. Based on OPM current charges, Secret level investigations can cost between $210-272 each, with TS/SCI level investigations costing an average of $3,959. These costs add up: Executive Branch agencies spent $1.6B in 2012 on Personnel Security Programs.[4]

---

[2] Individuals, such as those supporting the military or protecting our nation's most critical assets, may be determined eligible due to the sensitivity of their positions and the potential need for immediate access to classified information, but may not have access until the need arises

[3] By definition, military service members occupy National Security Positions. Therefore, all personnel entering the military are subject to the same investigations conducted for access to Secret information, even though they do not require a clearance eligibility determination.

[4] Agencies report security program expenditures annually to the Information Security Oversight Office. The "Personnel Security" category includes all expenses for investigations, reinvestigations, national agency record checks, clearance adjudications, and polygraphs.

Role of Contractors in Current Processes

The National Industrial Security Program

As mentioned, the same investigative and adjudicative standards apply to both Federal employees and contractors who receive clearances, as the work to protect our national security is no less critical when contractors perform the work. The National Industrial Security Program (NISP)[5] governs all aspects of sharing and safeguarding classified information with industry, including the means by which contractors receive and retain security clearances. The NISP directs contractors to limit requests for clearances to the minimal number of employees necessary for operational efficiency and consistent with contractual obligations. Contractors are also required to report any known adverse information concerning any of their cleared employees. However, in practice, it has been difficult to track compliance with this requirement. Further, these reporting requirements are not consistently required for contractors not holding security clearances, but who have access to Federal buildings and systems following a suitability determination.

Contractors as Investigative Service Providers

The Federal Government relies on a mixture of Federal and contractor personnel to operate government vetting programs. All decisions on whether to grant someone a security clearance are performed by Federal employees, consistent with government-wide OMB policy and the Federal Acquisition Regulation (FAR) on what work is deemed inherently governmental. Contractors are primarily used to provide both investigation and administrative support (e.g. collection of information such as local records). Utilizing contractors to perform these functions has given Federal Government agencies flexibility to adjust to ever-shifting demands in the investigative workload.

---

[5] In accordance with Executive Order 12829, the National Industrial Security Program is overseen by the Information Security Oversight Office on behalf of the Assistant to the President for National Security Affairs. The Department of Defense is executive agent, providing industrial security services for 26 Federal agencies.

KEY CONCLUSIONS AND RECOMMENDATIONS

This report identifies 13 major conclusions and recommendations, which aim to achieve three broad goals:

    A. Increase Availability of Critical Information to Improve Decision Making
    B. Reduce Inherent Risk in Current Processes
    C. Improve Enterprise Operations

While these recommendations do not address every potential problem encountered by security, suitability, and credentialing processes, implementing the following recommendations would dramatically improve performance across the Executive branch while addressing the most serious risks we face. This implementation effort will require resources, and is a major undertaking and would entail changes across the Federal Government - altering credentialing, suitability, and security clearance processes and approaches, and improving capabilities needed to execute this process in a high quality and efficient way. It will involve building new capabilities (e.g., scaling up key information technology investments, increasing data analytic capacity) and operating them in a more coordinated way across the Federal Government.

This report identifies the key changes that are needed and outlines an overall implementation approach, the details of which will be defined in a forthcoming implementation plan and timetable.[6] The PAC will take responsibility for driving implementation on a cross-agency basis and for delivering results.

As outlined in the recommendations below, we place emphasis on applying the same suitability and security standards to contractors and Federal employees, and ensuring that Federal oversight and accountability measures are in place to ensure compliance by contractors.

Section A: Increase the availability and quality of critical information to improve decision making

Federal agencies that conduct investigations and adjudications for credentialing, suitability, and national security must have access to relevant information from a variety of sources. Today, this presents considerable challenges, particularly in the areas of resources, automation, and policy barriers. We must overcome these challenges to reduce the gaps in our current processes and to develop a robust Continuous Evaluation (CE) process.

Conclusion A.1

Background investigations are missing critical information such as police reports of arrests.

This Review found that significant policy, technology, budgetary, and jurisdictional barriers prevent Federal or Federally-authorized background investigators from consistently accessing

---

[6] Timelines and dates outlined in this report are notional, and will be updated in the forthcoming implementation plan.

available Criminal History Records Information (CHRI) from state and local law enforcement agencies. Current law directs state and local law enforcement agencies to provide to CHRI to specified Federal agencies for the purposes of background investigations[7]. Yet when state or local law enforcement agencies fail to comply, it can result in incomplete data sources and substantial challenges for Federal Government investigations. Most critically, missing or incomplete CHRI could result in a favorable adjudication and granting of a security clearance because full and complete criminal history information was unobtainable. Appendix C summarizes the large number of denied requests for available CHRI by state.

Incomplete information can critically compromise the results of an investigation. For example, while the background investigation conducted on Aaron Alexis was compliant with OPM's established policies and practices, reliance on automated databases failed to reveal his use of a firearm, which led to his 2004 arrest. That information, though available in local records of the Seattle Police Department, was not provided to OPM and therefore, was not included as part of the investigation.

Recommendation A.1

Improve access to and availability of State and Local criminal records.

We recommend multiple measures to enhance Federal Government access to full and complete state and local criminal records. The PAC, in partnership with its member agencies and the Records Access Task Force, will review relevant statutes to determine if additional clarification is needed. The Task Force, comprised of key Federal agencies and a group of local law enforcement officials, was established on February 7, 2014[8]. If necessary, the PAC will recommend changes to current law to clarify and strengthen requirements for State and local law enforcement agencies to share CHRI information with Federal background investigators.

Additionally, the PAC and DOJ will explore options to ensure state and local entities comply with their obligations to make CHRI available, including leveraging related Federal funding to encourage cooperation with existing law, and support efforts to make this information available in automated form[9]. The majority of this work will be conducted by the recently mandated Records Access Task Force.

---

[7] 5 USC § 9101 – *Access to Criminal History Records for National Security Purposes*

[8] Establishing the Records Access Task Force is mandated by section 907(f) of the National Defense Authorization Act (NDAA) for Fiscal Year 2014, Pub. L. No. 113-66. The PAC Chair serves as Task Force Chair. Members include representatives from OPM, DoD, DNI, law enforcement agencies of DOJ and DHS, State and local law enforcement agencies and associations, and representatives of relevant State, local and Federal judicial systems that govern records access.

[9] DOJ and the PAC will work with the Compact Council to explore this recommendation. The Compact Council was established to facilitate authorized interstate criminal history exchanges for noncriminal justice purposes on a uniform basis, while permitting each State to effectuate its own dissemination policy within its own borders; and to allow Federal and State records to be provided expeditiously to governmental and nongovernmental agencies that use records in accordance with pertinent Federal and State law, while simultaneously enhancing the accuracy of the records and safeguarding the information contained therein from unauthorized disclosure or use.

Specific actions include:

- By April 2014, complete the study of specific areas for improving information sharing between the Federal Government and state and local law enforcement agencies through the Records Access Task Force, mandated by the National Defense Authorization Act (NDAA), and issue report.
- Within 90 days, reach agreement with DHS and DOJ on the appropriate Federal funding mechanisms to encourage cooperation or compliance with existing statutes to share data with Federal officials.
- Within 180 days, the PAC and DOJ will develop training and educational materials to help states and localities understand their legal obligations and the importance of data-sharing along with funding available to offset the cost of automation.

Conclusion A.2

Reportable information often goes unreported.

This Review found that clear and consistent requirements do not exist across government for employees or contractors to report, subsequent to their being hired or granted a clearance, information that could affect their continued fitness, suitability, or eligibility for Federal employment (e.g. criminal conduct, behaviors of concern), or their eligibility to access government facilities and IT systems. Neither is there consistent guidance in place to direct contractors or contract managers in the Federal Government to report noteworthy or derogatory information regarding employees. Compliance with such requirements is also critical. Such mechanisms are essential to ensure the safety of our workforce and protection of our most sensitive information. For example, even with reporting requirements in place, no reports were made of Aaron Alexis' multiple arrests or other personal conduct issues, either by the Navy or those in his company who were aware of his conduct.

Recommendation A.2

Clarify and expand requirements for reporting actions and behavior of employees and contractors to support decisions on access to facilities, classified/sensitive information, and IT systems.

We recommend that the PAC work with OPM and ODNI, in their roles as the Suitability and Security Executive Agents to propose and implement uniform reporting requirements for personnel (tiered by risk or eligibility level) that specify who is required to report certain events, behaviors, or observations. Once these uniform reporting requirements are established across the Executive branch, the PAC will work with the Executive branch agencies to ensure their implementation, including training for supervisors and employees to identify and report counterproductive work behaviors. Best practices by Federal agencies to facilitate self-reporting, such as the tools used by the Department of State should also be examined and if appropriate, applied Executive branch-wide.

Additionally, the PAC will work with the Office of Federal Procurement Policy to propose a change to the FAR to impose those applicable reporting requirements on contractors, and ensure that enforcement and accountability mechanisms are in place. The PAC will develop a dedicated work team to expedite progress on these changes.

Though not the primary subject of this Review, we note that mental health concerns pose a unique reporting challenge and we support Federal efforts to address this complex issue with sensitivity. To this end, revisions have been proposed to the Standard Form 86, National Security Questionnaire that focus on mental illness to the extent that it may impact an individual's judgment, reliability, and trustworthiness. We stress that it is important that agencies and contractors encourage employees to seek mental health treatment just as they would address any other health matter.

Specific actions include:

- Within 90 days, the PAC with work with ODNI and OMB to publish the revised Reporting Requirements policy for national security positions, and then establish a working group to expand those requirements to other suitability and contractor populations.
- The PAC will work with OMB's Office of Federal Procurement Policy and the Federal Acquisition Regulation Council to propose an appropriate rule to establish needed reporting requirements for the contractor population.
- In coordination with other Administration efforts, the PAC will establish a working group with participation from ODNI, OPM, DoD, the Department of Veterans Affairs (VA), the Department of Health and Human Services (HHS), and other appropriate Federal experts to further examine the relevant intersection of mental health issues and suitability and security reporting.

Conclusion A.3

Investigations occur too infrequently, creating unnecessary gaps in coverage.

This Review found that the current reinvestigation practices do not adequately reevaluate or appropriately mitigate risk within the security and suitability population. Lengthy periods between reinvestigations do not provide sufficient means to discover derogatory information that develops following the initial adjudication. Furthermore, resource constraints lead agencies to conduct fewer than the required number of reinvestigations.

A number of pilot tests are underway to explore and demonstrate CE capabilities. These CE pilots assess automated data checks from multiple sources (e.g., credit checks, social media, personnel records, and self-reporting records) that may reveal relevant information, prompting further investigation and enabling agencies to prioritize their efforts on those who appear to have the highest risk. For example, a DoD pilot tested the value and effectiveness of its Automated Continuous Evaluation System (ACES). That pilot sampled 3,370 Army service members, civilian employees, and contractor personnel, and identified that 21.7 percent of the tested population had previously unreported derogatory information that had developed since the last investigation, and 3 percent had serious derogatory information (e.g. financial issues, domestic abuse, drug abuse) that resulted in a revocation or suspension of a security clearance. This and other CE pilots provide compelling evidence for many benefits of this more continuous approach to background investigations.

Recommendation A.3

Accelerate the implementation of a standardized program of Continuous Evaluation (CE), ensure full integration with agency Insider Threat Programs, and reassess Periodic Reinvestigation intervals as appropriate.

We recommend the PAC establish and oversee an accelerated timetable for an integrated CE solution across all agencies and security levels. The current timetable calls for incremental implementation of CE with initial capability for the TS and TS/SCI level in 2014 and full implementation for these populations at that level in 2016. Several agencies are developing agency-specific CE capabilities that will be aligned and integrated with the ODNI CE solution, and the PAC intends to accelerate elements of those efforts.

The shift to CE will mean a different way of conducting investigations. As automation and other capabilities increase, we recommend driving toward a CE system that would, to the greatest extent possible, notify appropriate security officials of noteworthy events or incidents in near-real time. Furthermore, CE would access relevant data sources, in greater volume and with more frequency than our current system. By identifying issues between reinvestigations, CE will more frequently evaluate employees and contractors who are eligible for access to classified information by using periodic, random, and event-driven assessments to better resolve issues or identify risks to national security.

In addition, we would retain a periodic reinvestigation process, incorporating data gathered from CE. We will also take cases flagged by the continuous evaluation system for follow up investigation.

Implementing a system for continuous evaluation is resource intensive, and poses genuine technical and procedural challenges. Currently there is no government-wide capability, plan or design present in the investigative community to operate a data-driven architecture to collect, store, and share relevant information. An additional challenge will be the shift towards connectivity with external data sources to meet information collection needs. These technical and resource management challenges will require top-down direction and attention to resolve.

Success of the CE program will depend on a fully-integrated solution across government, which will eliminate inefficiency and avoid the expenses of duplicative systems. The PAC and ODNI will work with agencies across the Executive branch to develop the enterprise CE solution, while continuing to use lessons learned from pilots to test and validate key CE components and capabilities.

Specific actions include:

- By September 2014, ODNI will have an initial CE capability for the most sensitive TS and TS/SCI population with implementation for all TS and TS/SCI cleared personnel by 2016.
- By October 2014, DoD will expand its CE pilots to include a sample of 100,000 cleared military, DoD civilian, and contractor personnel updated on an ongoing basis from trusted data sources.
- By 2015, DoD will expand its CE capability to 225,000 personnel; increasing to 500,000 by the end of 2016 and 1 million during 2017. The FY 2015 cost projections for this

transition are approximately $53M. OMB will work with DoD to accommodate this within resource constraints.

- Through FY 2015 budget guidance, OMB required DOJ, Treasury, and DHS to identify agency funding to prioritize automation requirements for critical key databases that will be essential to service and enable CE capabilities. We are working to develop a cost estimate implementing CE in agencies other than DOD. OMB also required the DoD to fund development of the CE capability leveraging the ACES platform.

Conclusion A.4

Once implemented, the Revised 2012 Federal Investigative Standards (FIS) will significantly reduce gaps in current processes.

This Review found that the 2012 Federal Investigative Standards, which apply to employees and contractors working for the Executive branch, will provide needed improvements to the methods and scope of investigative processes. These aligned investigative processes enhance consistency and efficiency by building each successively higher level of investigation on the one below it, avoiding duplication. The standards provide additional information collection requirements at the Secret-level for information relevant to employment conduct, foreign activities and associates, and criminal history records. At the TS/SCI level, requirements include a comprehensive interview of the subject and other informants covering all areas of adjudicative significance.

Recommendation A.4

Accelerate implementation of elements of Revised Federal Investigative Standards (FIS) to address gaps identified in existing investigative processes.

We recommend acceleration of FIS implementation plans, with emphasis on improving access to key sources that will fill identified gaps in current practices. These include:

- Social Security Administration Check, which will provide adjudicators greater assurance of the subject's identity, potentially mitigating fraudulent submissions.
- Defense Management Data Center Check, which will provide adjudicators improved information regarding the characterization of military discharge.
- Scattered Castles, the Intelligence Community investigation and adjudication index database, which will provide adjudicators a full investigative history inclusive of the Intelligence Community conducted investigations.
- Full implementation of enhanced subject interviews when triggered by issues.
- Expanding the use of automated checks to verify citizenship, including measuring the effectiveness and adequacy of DHS SAVE[10] in light of other alternatives.

While the current FIS Implementation Plan projects full implementation of the standards across government by 2017, it is necessary to accelerate the critical areas outlined above. As part of the

---

[10]The Systematic Alien Verification for Entitlements (SAVE) Program is designed to assist benefit-granting agencies in determining an applicant's immigration status, and thereby ensure that only entitled applicants receive Federal aid.

overall implementation planning efforts, the PAC will develop a timeline to prioritize and accelerate these enhancements.

Specific actions include:

- By April 2014, Security and Suitability Executive Agents will submit the comprehensive FIS Implementation Plan to the PAC, including detailed timelines and cost estimates where feasible to fill gaps in current practice.
- The PAC will work with the Executive Agents and agencies to accelerate implementation of the critical checks above to enable the acceleration of full implementation across government to 2016.

Section B: Reduce risks that are inherent in our current processes

Beyond the foregoing information gaps, our review process identified the need to improve the consistency of decision-making across the Executive Branch, increase the timeliness and completeness of reinvestigations, and improve the oversight and approach to measuring the quality of investigative work. Our recommendations form an integrated approach to address these risks. The PAC will develop detailed plans to accelerate implementation of these recommendations.

Conclusion B.1

The current backlog of Periodic Reinvestigations - especially for our most sensitive populations - creates vulnerabilities.

This Review found that there is a significant backlog of overdue periodic reinvestigations within agencies across the Executive branch, principally due to resource constraints. Specifically the most recent data show that roughly 22 percent of the population eligible for access to classified information at the TS or TS/SCI level was outdated, and no reinvestigation had been requested.[11] This backlog poses unacceptable risk, leaving the U.S. Government potentially uninformed as to behavior that poses a security or counterintelligence concern.

Recommendation B.1

Reduce Periodic Reinvestigation backlog using a risk-based approach.

We recommend that the Security Executive Agent develop a strategy and process that reduces the risk posed by the Periodic Reinvestigation backlog across government. For example, prioritizing Periodic Reinvestigation submissions by risk – based on both the nature of the position held by the individuals and the results of automated records checks — can help identify individuals of potential concern. Prior CE pilots have demonstrated that automated records checks, like credit reports and criminal checks through FBI's Rapback system, are readily

---

[11] This figure represents updated data as of March 2014

accessible and cost effective and could be used in the near future to flag individuals who should have highest priority for Periodic Reinvestigations.

Specific actions include:

- By April 2014, OMB will distribute to the President's Management Council (comprised primarily of agency Deputy Secretaries) the results of agencies' compliance with the DNI's October 2013 memorandum that directs agencies to use a risk-based approach to identify high risk populations and prioritize reinvestigations that have come due or are overdue.
- Within 180 days, the Security Executive Agent will determine a near-term government-wide strategy for agencies to identify high risk populations through the use of automated records checks (e.g. derogatory credit or criminal activity) and prioritize overdue investigations based upon risk posed by job responsibilities and access in order to reduce risks posed by potential insider threats.

Conclusion B.2

Growth in the number of clearance-holders increases costs and exposes classified national security information, often at very sensitive levels, to an increasingly large population.

This Review found that the large number of individuals currently eligible to hold a security clearance has significantly increased both risk and costs. Executive branch policy expressly directs agencies to minimize the number of individuals with eligibility for access to classified information to that required to conduct agency functions. It also expressly prohibits requesting eligibility in excess of actual requirements. Despite these policies, 5.1 million employees and contractors were eligible for security clearances as of October 2013, as shown in Table 1 above.

Large numbers of clearances, especially those at higher levels, increase investigative program costs. As stated above, based on OPM data a Top Secret/SCI investigation costs approximately $3959, while a Secret investigation costs between $210-272. To illustrate one of many examples, Appendix D demonstrates that for the DoD, the number of Top Secret/SCI investigations increased 42 percent between 2005 and 2013, resulting in an increase in over $179M in program costs.

Recommendation B.2

Reduce total population of 5.1M Secret and TS/SCI clearance holders to minimize risk of access to sensitive information and reduce cost.

We recommend that, consistent with guidance promulgated by the Security Executive Agent, Federal agencies conduct a comprehensive review of their positions to validate that each government employee and each contractor who has been deemed eligible for access to classified information continues to require such eligibility to support their agency's mission. These efforts will not only validate that individuals with access to classified information have a need to know, but may also reduce the classification level for which they need access, thereby reducing the cost of Periodic Reinvestigations. The cost savings will enable agencies to repurpose limited resources to accelerate efforts such as transitioning to continuous evaluation, as appropriate. The

Security Executive Agent shall ensure full compliance with this guidance and report results to the PAC, once reviews are complete.

Specific actions include:

- By April, 2014, OMB will distribute to the President's Management Council, the results of agency compliance with October 2013 guidance from the DNI to review all positions determine whether it continues to require access to classified material.
- Within 90 days, OPM and ODNI will work with OMB to finalize a joint regulation to refine the designation of national security positions and more accurately align investigations with risks.

Conclusion B.3

Performance measures for investigation and adjudication quality are neither standardized nor implemented consistently.

This Review found that the current performance measures for investigative and adjudicative quality involve disparate and difficult to integrate data sources. Measuring and ensuring quality continues to be a challenge, as aspects of what makes a case acceptable can vary. For example, not all agree whether an investigation meets quality standards if it is missing information that is beyond the ability of an investigator to collect (e.g. the subject interview cannot be conducted when the subject is in a war zone, or law enforcement agencies won't conduct record checks). This complicates the use of the quality tools that exist today. These issues of quality and metrics were also noted in recent testimony by the Government Accountability Office (GAO) on personnel security clearances (GAO-14-187T). As mentioned previously, the Review found that the current practice of utilizing contractors to conduct background investigations is appropriate and consistent with regulations.

However, improvements are needed in the areas of contract oversight and quality metrics going forward. Recently, OPM federalized all of the second level quality reviews (after delivery of the contractor file to OPM), following a whistleblower lawsuit, joined by DOJ alleging fraud in the first level quality review process by one of OPM's contract investigative services providers.

Recommendation B.3

Accelerate the development of quality standards and implementation of consistent measures and metrics for investigations and adjudications, and improve the quality of existing oversight mechanisms for Federal and contract investigators, and Federal adjudicators.

We recommend accelerating PAC activities to implement consistently-defined quality measures, metrics, and tools. The PAC will oversee and measure progress of the work of the Security and Suitability Executive Agents and the Under Secretary of Defense for Intelligence, being carried out by the Quality Assessment Working Group (QAWG). The PAC will ensure the successful development of standardized tools to measure and report investigative and adjudicative quality, and will hold agencies accountable for implementing the standards and tools.

In conjunction with these important measurement tools, effective oversight and management are important to ensuring proper application of tools and satisfaction of standards. For investigations, quality assurance reviews by appropriate personnel prior to delivery of the investigation to the agency, in depth random sampling quality reviews, and integrity assurance re-contact programs are critical. All investigating agencies should examine their processes and ensure these oversight mechanisms and other quality tools are in place to optimize quality and ensure integrity throughout the process. These oversight mechanisms should apply to Federal employees and contractors alike.

Specific actions include:

- By June 2014, the Executive Agents will issue for PAC approval consistent government-wide quality standards for investigations for the first time and begin collecting quality metrics based on these standards by October 2014.
- By September 2014, the QAWG will develop a quality assessment tool for investigations.
- Ongoing, the PAC and the Security and Suitability Executive Agent will work with agencies to develop adjudicative quality standards, critically examine the existing process, assess the adequacy of oversight mechanisms in place, and share best practices.

Conclusion B.4

The current investigation and adjudication process frequently fails to detect false information supplied by applicants.

Credentialing, suitability, and national security vetting processes all rely on information submitted about the applicant. However, this Review found that falsification of suitability and security questionnaires is a frequent occurrence, and our current processes lack the ability to easily detect when applicants provide false information. Furthermore, there is no Federal level guidance to provide adjudicators consistent or clear paths of action when some form of false information is provided by the applicant.

The application is usually completed by the applicant in the electronic questionnaire system (e-QIP). For some categories, such as military recruits and contractor personnel, the application is completed by third parties (recruiters or company security officers) using e-QIP interface systems. This introduces risk to questionnaire integrity, and it makes identifying and acting on falsification more difficult. Personal accountability cannot be established because it is difficult to determine if the applicant is being deceptive, or if the third party was at fault.

However, even when falsification is uncovered, it is not treated consistently. As reviews of the Aaron Alexis investigation revealed, Alexis did not admit criminal and traffic offenses and indebtedness when he completed the security clearance application (Standard Form 86, *National Security Questionnaire*). These falsifications were detected during the original investigations, but did not result in an unfavorable adjudication.

Recommendation B.4

Improve detection of and response to applicant falsification in current processes.

We recommend the Suitability and Security Executive Agents take several measures (jointly as needed) to improve the detection of and response to applicant falsification.

- Develop standard criteria and procedures to ensure agencies respond appropriately to falsification in all types of security clearance, suitability, and credentialing adjudications.
- Develop and implement improved investigator and adjudicator training to better identify and act upon falsification.
- Develop policy and procedures to address problems that occur when third parties are involved in completing suitability and security questionnaires on behalf of applicants (e.g. military recruiters).
- Develop better tools to validate self-reported information against other available independent sources (e.g. social media, credit, or human resources data).

The Executive Agents will provide input to the PAC implementation plan specifying the specific timeline for implementation of these measures.

Specific actions include:

- Within 180 days, the PAC will work with DoD and OPM to expand standardized e-QIP for military and contractor personnel to address third party influence/falsification.
- Within 18 months, the PAC will develop IT capabilities and other tools to enable detection of falsification that can be integrated with existing systems.

Conclusion B.5

Credentialing decisions that enable physical access to government facilities or IT systems are applied in an inconsistent way.

This Review found that the guidelines for both suitability and security clearance determinations include criteria that address workplace safety and security (see Appendix E for Gap Analysis). However, the minimum standards to grant credentials that enable physical access to government facilities and logical access to government IT systems (Final Credentialing Standards for Issuing Personal Identity Verification Cards under HSPD-12) focus primarily on whether an individual is who they claim to be, and if they have a nexus to terrorism. Additional factors to be considered in determining whether that individual presents other risks to workplace safety or national security are not pursued.

The Final Credentialing Standards, established in 2008 contain supplemental criteria that address these additional risks. Because these supplemental standards set forth by OPM are currently available but not mandatory, there is inconsistency for this level of vetting. For example, approximately half of the contract employees investigated by OPM last year were adjudicated using the minimum adjudicative standards as opposed to the supplemental standards. The supplemental standards are minimal in cost and reduce risk, and there would be significant value in having one unified set of standards that includes the supplemental material.

Recommendation B.5

Establish new Government-wide adjudication requirements for credentials[12] issued to include the currently optional OPM supplementary standards.

We recommend the adoption of the OPM supplemental standards for credentialing discussed above as the minimum required by all Federal agencies. To accomplish this recommendation, the President would have to direct OPM to require unified criteria for issuance of access credentials for all employees and contractors who hold PIV (Personal Identification Verification) cards. Such criteria should be consistent with OPM's suitability factors and make mandatory current optional supplemental standards.

Specific actions include:

- Within 180 days, the PAC will identify the specific timing of actions to accomplish, including mandating supplemental credentialing criteria to apply to all persons with access to government facilities and information systems, including modifications to the FAR.

Conclusion B.6

The lack of clarity on whether or how to suspend credentials creates vulnerabilities to personnel-related threats.

This Review found that there are not explicit criteria or procedures to suspend an individual's PIV card, as opposed to revoking it. This creates confusion about an agency's or contractor's options when it is investigating potential concerns about an employee or contractor, leading to inaction or delay in action, when an issue concerning character or conduct emerges after the credential has been issued. Consequently, government agencies could unknowingly grant physical access (based on PIV card reciprocity) to individuals undergoing adverse administrative actions.

Recommendation B.6

Revise the Final Credentialing Standards to establish a suspension mechanism.

We recommend that OPM revise the Final Credentialing Standards to expressly reference the criteria and procedures for immediately suspending credentials, when appropriate. These standard procedures will allow an agency to take timely action to protect its workforce and facilities while it determines if a credentialed individual poses a threat. It should also ensure that agencies issue a formal revocation, or otherwise resolve the suspension, as well as provide for a review process.

---

[12] Homeland Security Presidential Directive 12 was issued on August 12, 2004 by President George W. Bush. HSPD-12 calls for a mandatory, government-wide standard for secure and reliable forms of ID (or PIV cards – Personal Identification Verification) issued by the Federal Government to its employees and employees of federal contractors for access to federally-controlled facilities and networks.

Specific actions include:

- Within 180 days, OPM will issue additional guidance to outline the criteria and procedures for suspension of PIV credentials.

Section C: Improve Enterprise Operations

The existing Executive branch agency operations for credentialing, suitability, and security clearances are complex and implementing the recommendations found in this report necessitates active leadership and continued involvement of the PAC. The PAC should lead a comprehensive enterprise approach to define and deliver against an accelerated implementation plan. This plan should address the recommendations above, as well as supporting actions needed in the areas of information technology, performance management, strategic sourcing, resource planning, and cost analysis. The PAC and the agencies included in its membership should be accountable for delivering these improvement in a timely, efficient, and high quality way.

Conclusion C.1

The Security and Suitability Performance Accountability Council needs a more active posture to achieve and sustain successful reforms.

Over the past six years, PAC leadership drove adoption of several key reforms, ultimately meeting statutory requirements for timeliness and getting the government's largest personnel security program, DoD's, removed from the GAO high risk list. More recently, however, PAC activity decreased. This lack of a coordinated Executive branch-wide effort has prevented the Federal Government from maintaining the pace of improvements.

Recommendation C.1

Recompose the PAC to actively manage and oversee enterprise issues

We recommend that, going forward, the PAC resume its highly active role in coordinating and ensuring full implementation of these recommendations. We also propose adding PAC members with new expertise necessary to establish and oversee strategies for investment, IT development, performance management, and reciprocity.

Specifically, we recommend that the PAC:

- Immediately recompose the PAC membership, the PAC Chair (OMB/DDM) will regularly convene senior leaders to hold them accountable for implementation as well as bring in agencies whose capabilities are critical to success (e.g., DOJ, FBI, DHS, State, Treasury).
- Immediately establish a PAC Program Management Office (PMO) to focus on implementation of this Report's recommendations.
- Immediately add new expert members, the PAC Chair will engage the Federal CIO and or OSTP/Chief Technology Officer for support to the assessment of current IT capabilities across this "line of business" and to develop IT strategy for long term needs of suitability and security processes.

As part of the FY 2015 Budget, OMB will also establish $3 million for the PMO, which will be transferred from six major agencies by the end of calendar year 2014 and is not dependent on Congressional action. The PMO will report directly to the PAC Chair.

Existing PAC members OMB, ODNI, OPM and DoD remain critical to coordinating, monitoring and achieving needed improvements. Beyond the current involvement of security and suitability communities, it is necessary to invoke subject matter expertise and government-wide processes for resource management, investment planning and information technology development to ensure new capabilities are developed in the most efficient and timely manner.

The PAC Chair, in consultation with the Security and Suitability Executive Agents, will identify personnel to provide for the enhanced governance, as well as other dedicated resources to support implementation efforts. They will also leverage expertise across government and outside to advise on the technical aspects of implementation, particularly with respect to CE which is highly data intensive, and requires a continuous learning approach. The PAC will also leverage the considerable dedicated agency resources that are focused on suitability and security clearance activities and process improvements to drive the work already underway within agencies and do so in a highly coordinated fashion.

Specific actions include:

- The PAC will immediately identify new members and meet as reconstituted within 30 days of this report.
- The PAC Chair (OMB/DDM) will convene members at least quarterly, and hold senior leaders accountable for implementation as well as bring in agencies whose capabilities are critical to success (e.g., DOJ, FBI, DHS, State, Treasury).
- The PAC will immediately establish a PMO to provide full-time effort and expertise on tasks of implementation. PMO membership shall include a minimum of 1 FTE from each of the following: OMB, DoD, ODNI, OPM, DHS, DOJ, and FBI.
- The PAC Chair will propose funding for the PMO through the FY15 budget ($500,000 annually per PMO member agency) for implementation efforts continuing at least through FY20 to ensure sustained momentum of these reform efforts.
- The PAC Chair will engage the Federal CIO and or OSTP/Chief Technology Officer for support to the assessment of current IT capabilities across this "line of business" and to develop IT strategy for long term needs of suitability and security processes.

Conclusion C.2

Greater focus is needed to develop enterprise-wide information technology capabilities.

This Review found that previous PAC action stopped short of strategies and actions needed to develop enterprise-wide information technology capabilities to modernize, integrate, and automate agency capabilities and retire legacy systems. Absent a strategy for integrated IT capabilities, agencies created disparate tools designed only to meet their specific requirements. Examples include differing systems for electronic application, investigative and/or adjudicative case management, incompatible databases for storage, reference and sharing of investigative actions and adjudicative decisions, among others. Such tools do not enable satisfactory collaboration, nor ensure efficiency of processes, a key concern in the current resource environment. The recommendations in this report (e.g. sharing data, automating access to state and local criminal records, and bringing CE capability online) largely depend on fixing this fragmented approach with enterprise-wide solutions.

Recommendation C.2

Develop and execute enterprise Reform IT strategy to ensure interoperability, operationalize CE, automate suitability processes, and improve sharing of relevant information.

We recommend that the PAC adopt medium and long-range plans to develop an appropriate Executive branch-wide IT architecture for the security, suitability, and credentialing line of business. Developing a CE capability is highly IT intensive and will require appropriate resources. Capitalizing on lessons learned from ongoing ODNI, DoD, and OPM efforts to develop CE will be critical.

This IT strategy should address ways to leverage technology, avoid duplicative investments, and promote reciprocity, government-wide efficiency, and the effective reuse of investigative and adjudicative decisions, including but not limited to:

- Means to provide real-time access to authoritative enterprise data on the conduct of investigations and the adjudicative decisions from across the government
- Electronic accessibility of Federal, State, and local government and criminal justice agency records
- Means to operationalize CE in the near and long term
- Capability for individuals to continuously update their electronic security forms
- An enterprise approach for case management, to include IT systems
- Incorporation of authorized and relevant new data sources, to include social media

Any such strategy must ensure system include capabilities to safeguard individual privacy and civil liberties, consistent with the needs of national security and workplace safety.

Specific actions include:

- Within 180 days, the PAC will conduct benchmarking of similar Government screening technologies (DHS, TSA, National Counterterrorism Center), as well as benchmarking of commercial solutions for risk-management and rules-based automation of previously manual workflows.
- Within 180 days, the PAC will develop and approve the reform IT strategy. The strategy will include medium and long term plans and will also include a clear, integrated proposal for the 2016 budget.

Conclusion C.3

There is a lack of enterprise Security/Suitability/Credentialing process cost analysis, investment planning for major reform initiatives, and automated records collection capability to enable transition to needed end-to-end automated capabilities.

This Review found that there is no central means to collect, analyze, manage or oversee spending for suitability and security processes across the Executive branch. Neither is there a program to link that spending to prescribed goals for performance, or the needs for investment in information technology or workforce development.

Given the current decentralized approach, certain decisions made at the agency level may increase Executive-branch wide risks. For example, in recent years, fiscal constraints limited timely reinvestigations, resulting in a backlog that has increased risk across the Federal Government.

Recommendation C.3

Establish mechanisms to manage and oversee government-wide spending for suitability and security processes.

We recommend that, in partnership with OMB, the PAC institute practices to manage enterprise costs, to conduct analysis ensuring investments to support the IT strategy, and to drive efficiencies in the overall system. This will include an examination of the role of contractors and how to structure contractor relationships to ensure incentives and control mechanisms are optimized for the critical nature of these activities. Ensuring oversight and quality control with respect to work by contractors will be essential to this study. We will begin by meeting the requirements of the 2014 NDAA to assess the efficiency and quality of current approaches. This effort is already underway, and due to be completed later this spring

Specific actions include:

- Within 12 months, the PAC will establish a mechanism to collect baseline financial data on security and suitability activities.
- Build on the conclusions of the NDAA efficiency and quality study to develop an ongoing capability to evaluate costs of suitability and security activities; identify opportunities for improvement; and provide agency information on quality and timeliness.

IMPLEMENTATION AND NEXT STEPS

This Review's recommendations reflect both new priorities driven by recent security incidents, as well as the need to accelerate progress on plans from ongoing reform efforts. Pending the approval of these recommendations, the PAC, chaired by OMB's Deputy Director for Management will actively manage and monitor implementation for all recommendations, reporting at regular intervals to the President on progress and to highlight emerging needs and recommend further action. The first such report, delivered within the next 90 days, will provide more detailed action plans for implementation of each recommendation of the review. We will coordinate these actions with other initiatives underway at your direction. Additionally, we will ensure that we work with OIRA to follow appropriate processes, including the regulatory review process.

As part of our efforts to ensure implementation efforts are sustained throughout this Administration and beyond, we will establish a four-year Cross Agency Priority Goal as part of the FY 2015 Budget focused on Insider Threat and Security Clearance Reform. As one of only 15 cross agency goals, this will ensure consistent attention from senior leadership. We will also name the Director of National Intelligence, the Director of the Office of Personnel Management and the Special Assistant to the President and Cybersecurity Coordinator as co-goal leaders responsible for driving implementation. OMB and the PAC will review progress every quarter against metrics and milestones as well as report progress publicly, as appropriate, to ensure accountability. These goals will be released on March 10, 2014.

These detailed implementation plans for each recommendation will take into account the appropriate stakeholders, timeframes, and actions. Where recommendations call for new initiatives, challenges may include: unplanned expenditures and as yet undetermined funding sources; potential policy or statutory barriers which must be altered before operational changes can be put in place; need to identify/provide information technology expertise/resources where it may not be sufficient.

The PAC Principals intend to work together to provide a consistent Administration communication strategy to agency, Congressional, industry and public stakeholders. This will include how we communicate with the families affected by prior incidents. We will also study the need to identify and move forward with a legislative agenda to better enable execution of these recommendations.

APPENDICES

A. PAC, Executive Agents, Agency Heads Roles and Responsibilities
B. 5-Tiered Investigative Model
C. Criminal History Denials by State
D. Increase in DoD Investigative Costs based on Volume
E. Gaps in Vetting Workplace Safety Issues

Appendix A: Roles and Responsibilities

THE PERFORMANCE ACCOUNTABILITY COUNCIL

The Performance Accountability Council is ultimately responsible to the President for "driving implementation of the reform effort, ensuring accountability by agencies, ensuring the Suitability Executive Agent and the Security Executive Agent align their respective processes, and sustaining reform momentum." In accordance with Executive Order 13467, the Deputy Director for Management of the Office of Management and Budget serves as the Chair of the PAC. The Chair has authority, direction, and control over the Council's functions, and may designate officials from additional agencies to serve as members of the Council. Roles and responsibilities of the PAC include:

- Ensuring alignment of suitability, security, and contractor fitness as appropriate;
- Holding agencies accountable for implementation of suitability, security, and contractor fitness processes and procedures;
- Establishing requirements for enterprise information technology;
- Establishing annual goals and progress metrics and preparing annual reports on results;
- Ensuring and overseeing the development of tools and techniques for enhancing background investigations and making eligibility determinations;
- Arbitrating disparities in procedures between Suitability and Security Executive Agents;
- Ensuring the sharing of best practices; and
- Advising the Suitability Executive Agent and the Security Executive Agent on polices affecting the alignment of investigation and adjudication and effective implementation.

In accordance with its responsibility to coordinate and drive reform implementation, the PAC establishes requirements for enterprise information technology needed to achieve the goals of modernizing processes and meeting performance goals. It does so in partnership with lead implementing agencies; OPM, DoD and the ODNI on behalf of the Intelligence Community, who are responsible for managing and modernizing the family of systems that supply Federal-level capabilities necessary to achieve the goal of end-to-end technology. The PAC also guides the direction of IT modernization efforts of agencies to ensure their systems, particularly those for the management of investigative and adjudicative cases, will comply and interoperate with the enterprise systems and ensure that record repositories automate their information so they can be accessed and shared rapidly across the Executive Branch.

THE OFFICE OF DIRECTOR NATIONAL INTELLIGENCE

EO 13467 designated the Director of National Intelligence as the Security Executive Agent. The Security Executive Agent is one of two permanent members of the PAC. As the Security Executive Agent, the Director of National Intelligence has the following roles and responsibilities:

- Directing the oversight of investigations and determinations of eligibility for access to classified information or eligibility to hold a sensitive position;
- Developing uniform and consistent policies and procedures for effective, efficient and timely completion of national security investigation and adjudication;
- Providing the final authority to designate agencies to conduct investigations of persons for access to classified information or eligibility to hold a sensitive position;
- Providing the final authority to designate agencies to adjudicate persons for security clearance;
- Ensuring reciprocal recognition of eligibility for access to classified information;
  Arbitrating and resolving disputes among agencies involving the reciprocity of investigations and

determinations to access classified information or occupy a sensitive position; and

- Prescribing under EO 12968, as amended, standards for investigating, reinvestigating, continuously evaluating, and adjudicating eligibility for access to classified information.

In addition, Sections 2.4 and 3 of EO 13467 reserved and reaffirmed the DNI's existing authorities. These include:

- Prescribing uniform standards, procedures, and guidelines for access to sensitive compartmented information (Section 102A, National Security Act of 1947, as amended, EO 12333).

THE OFFICE OF PERSONNEL MANAGEMENT

EO 13467 designated the Director of the Office of Personnel Management as the Suitability Executive Agent. The Suitability Executive Agent is one of the two permanent members of the PAC. As the Suitability Executive Agent, the Director of the Office of Personnel Management has the following roles and responsibilities:

- Developing and implementing uniform and consistent policies and procedures to ensure the effective, efficient, and timely completion of investigation and adjudications relating to determinations of suitability and eligibility for logical and physical access.

In addition, Sections 2.4 and 3 of EO 13467 reserved and reaffirmed the OPM Director's existing authorities. These include:

- Executing, administering, and enforcing civil service laws, rules, and regulations, and regulating and enforcing statutes and executive orders conferring responsibilities on OPM, including those concerning suitability and security (5 U.S.C. 1103, 1104; EO 10577);
- Conducting security, suitability, and credentialing investigations for the competitive service (and for the excepted service upon request); conducting investigations for the Department of Defense (including security clearance investigations for Defense contractors and the Armed Forces); and conducting reimbursable investigations (EO 10450, 10577; PL 108-136; 5 U.S.C. 1304, 9101);
- Maintaining an index of security investigations; approving reemployment of persons who have been summarily removed on national security grounds; conducting an ongoing review of agencies' personnel security programs; and reporting compliance to the National Security Council (EO 10450);
- Establishing suitability standards, conducting suitability adjudications, and taking suitability actions for the competitive service (EO 10577); and
- Conducting oversight of agencies' compliance with the civil service rules, and of their performance of delegated investigative and adjudicative authorities. (5 U.S.C. 1104, 1303; EO 10577).

Further, under a subsequent order, EO 13488, OPM prescribes fitness reciprocity requirements for contract and excepted service employment, reinvestigate requirements for contract and excepted service employment, and reinvestigate requirements for public trust positions.

THE DEPARTMENT OF DEFENSE

DoD generates 90% of the security investigation requirements in the Executive Branch, and 70% of Security and Suitability investigation requirements when combined. DoD is also responsible for making the Suitability and Security eligibility determinations associated with those investigations, and has responsibility for industrial security and counterintelligence functions. Although DoD is not assigned a statutory role in Security and Suitability reform, Section 3 of EO 13467 reaffirms DOD's industrial security role under EO 12829, as amended. In addition, DoD, along with OPM and the DNI, is a key component and participant of the reform effort. Pilot the full suite of Automated Records Checks to inform Executive Branch policies, and;

- Demonstrate Continuous Evaluation using ARC capabilities to inform Executive Branch CE policies.

AGENCIES WITH RECORDS REPOSITORY RESPONSIBILITIES

E.O. 13467 (Part 2, Section 2.1 (b)) calls for a system of investigations, which "shall employ updated and consistent methods…and end-to-end automation to the extent practicable, and ensure that relevant information maintained by agencies can be accessed and shared rapidly across the Executive Branch." Federal agencies with record repositories are responsible for:

- Following PAC standards for automating records for exchange of investigative record requests and responses;
- Automating record repositories;
- Developing an automated means to exchange all record requests; and
- Establishing a means for tracking timeliness of record requests and final record responses between themselves and other record repositories.

AGENCY HEADS

The heads of agencies that make security and suitability determinations must conduct their security and suitability programs in accordance with applicable statutes, executive orders, and regulations. Agencies are also fully engaged and held accountable for implementing reform policies, processes and procedures. Agency heads may participate in the PAC as designated by the Council. To the extent consistent with law, Agency heads are specifically responsible for following Executive Agent security and suitability guidance in:

- Implementing security and suitability policies;
- Implementing reform procedures and incorporating IT capabilities requirements to the extent practical as appropriate to satisfy reform goals;
- Reporting on performance progress as required by the Executive Agents and the Deputy Director of Management and Budget;
- Cooperating in oversight and audit efforts; and
- Planning and resourcing to satisfy reform performance requirements.

Appendix B: Five-Tiered Investigative Model

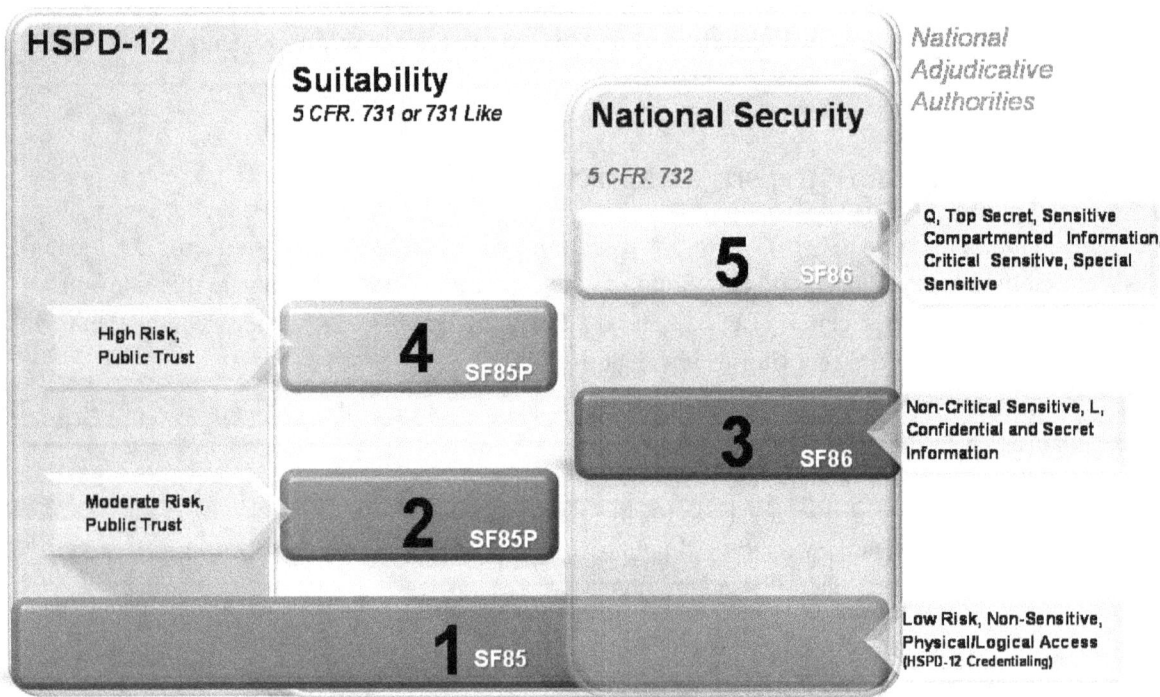

Appendix C: Denial of Criminal History Record Information by State (FY13 data)

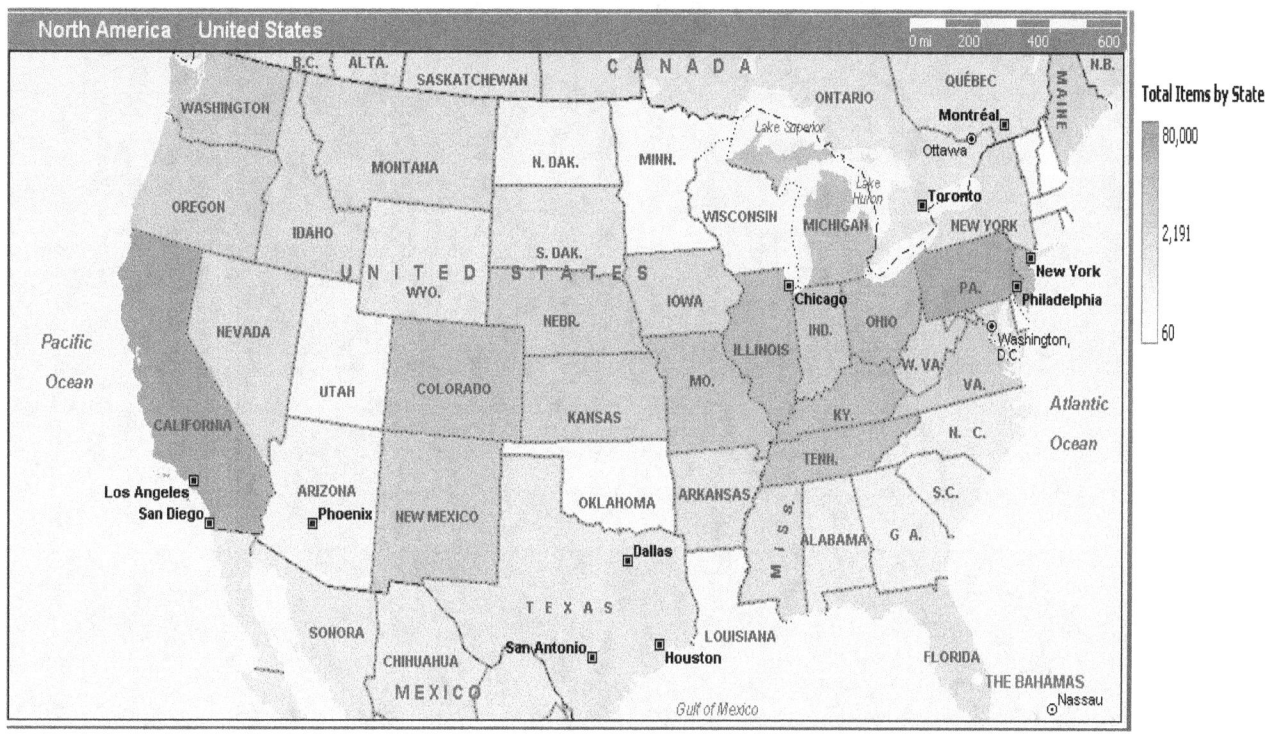

Appendix D: Increase in Investigative Costs Based on DoD Volume

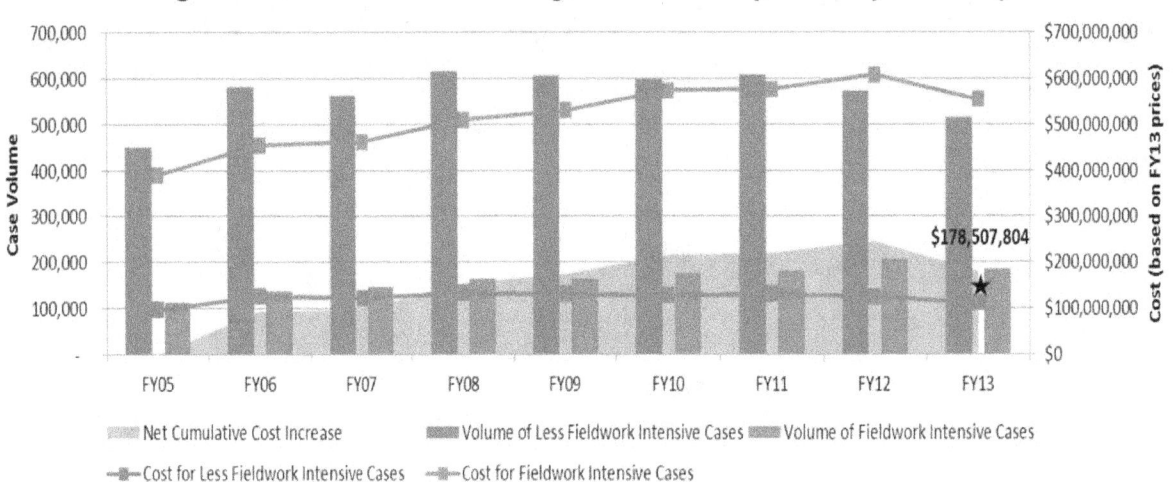

Significant Cost Drivers – Investigation Mix – Requested by DoD Only

Investigation Type		FY05	FY06	FY07	FY08	FY09	FY10	FY11	FY12	FY13	% Change FY05 to FY13
Less Fieldwork Intensive	Total	450,505	581,451	563,463	615,437	606,926	598,067	608,515	572,295	515,900	15%
	Cost Based on FY13 Prices	$96,540,724	$126,165,959	$122,258,252	$132,434,773	$130,100,938	$128,066,776	$130,633,918	$124,269,698	$111,792,461	16%
Fieldwork Intensive	Total	113,097	135,954	147,777	164,330	163,718	175,940	181,190	205,585	184,775	63%
	Cost Based on FY13 Prices	$390,243,657	$454,016,638	$462,175,815	$509,381,612	$530,464,702	$574,217,534	$576,315,714	$607,880,308	$553,499,724	42%
Total Cost		$486,784,381	$580,182,597	$584,434,067	$641,816,385	$660,565,640	702,284,310	$706,949,632	$732,150,006	$665,292,185	37%

Appendix E: Gap in Vetting Workplace Safety Issues

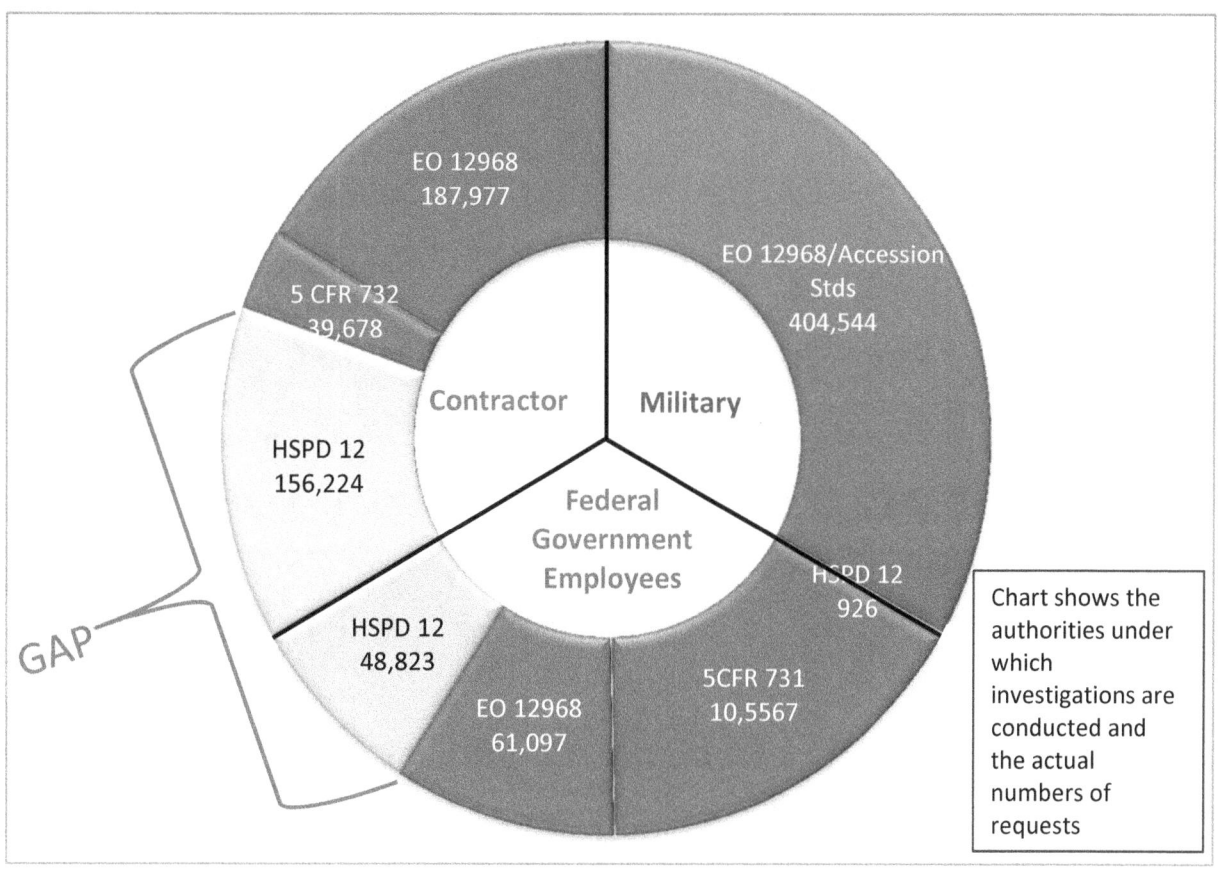